EUDIST PRAYERBOOK SERIES:
VOLUME 2

More Than Just 50 Beads

ROSARY MEDITATIONS FOR THE LITURGICAL YEAR

by St. John Eudes

Translated from
Oremos con San Juan Eudes
by Fr. Alvaro Torres Fajardo, CJM
Cali, Colombia, Padres Eudistas.
©2005 Used with permission

Translations by
Thomas Merton
and
Steven S. Marshall

Cover image: a 40 ton marble statue of St. John Eudes in St. Peter's Basilica. Carved in 1932 by Silvio Silva, this is one of 39 large statues around the Basilica's nave and transepts honoring the founders of great religious orders.

ISBN: 978-0-9979114-1-1

Published by

744 Sonrisa Street
Solana Beach, CA 92075
www.eudistsusa.org

Table of Contents

Introduction

For the recitation of the Rosary

"For Fr. Eudes himself, the Rosary was a regular habit. It was his daily exercise. He always wore one at his belt, pleased to know that everyone could see how much he gloried in his devotion to it." [1]

The Rosary is a spiritual exercise which unites religion to daily life. In it, we unite ourselves to Mary by meditating on the mysteries of our Lord Jesus, the Son of God. The Church advises us to pray it both personally and communally. A particular text of scripture may be chosen to deepen our meditation on the mystery in consideration. It is also possible to add a phrase for meditation which illuminates the practical aspect of the mystery being prayed.

To go along with the traditional mysteries: Joyful, Sorrowful and Glorious, St. John Paul II added the Luminous Mysteries, or Mysteries of Divine Light.

Being a private devotion, it is also possible, on one's own initiative, to recite it in the spirit of the current liturgical season. We will offer several possibilities as useful suggestions for a fruitful recitation.

In addition, you will find a set of other Rosary devotions which St. John Eudes himself composed and gave to his followers. His intention was for these new rosaries to help deepen our devotion to the Trinity and to the Blessed Virgin Mary.

Fr. Alvaro Torres Fajardo CJM
Cali, Colombia
August 19, 2005
325th Anniversary of St. John Eudes' entry into Eternal Life

---

[1]   Fr. Pierre Herambourg CJM, *St. John Eudes: A Spiritual Portrait* (Newman Press: Westminster, MD), p.113-114.

Praying the Rosary With St. John Eudes

[These are excerpts from *The Life and the Kingdom of Jesus: A Treatise on Christian Perfection for Use by Clergy or Laity,* Translated from the French by A Trappist Father in The Abbey of Our Lady of Gethsémani and published by Kennedy & Sons in New York, 1946.

Why We Pray the Rosary, and With What Dispositions

Only mental blindness or prodigious ignorance of the things of God could lead us to doubt that the devotion of the Rosary of the Most Blessed Virgin came from heaven and was inspired by God. It is approved and practiced by the universal Church; it contains the holiest prayers anyone could possibly say, the *Our Father*, the *Hail Mary*, and the *Creed*, and it is a most excellent means of honoring the first mystery of the life of Jesus, the greatest wonder God ever accomplished on earth: the miracle of the Incarnation of the Son of God in the most holy Virgin Mary. This incomparable wonder and admirable mystery, which perpetually enraptures all heaven and is there adored without interruption, should be adored just as incessantly on earth. This is because it took place on earth for the benefit of the dwellers of the earth, and because the Church Militant is bound to follow and imitate the Church Triumphant in heaven.

The mystery of the Incarnation is indeed continually adored on earth in several different ways, especially by the three *Hail Marys* of the *Angelus*, repeated three times a day at the sound of a bell, in the morning, at noon and in the evening, and by the recitation of the *Rosary*, made up of fifty-three *Hail Marys*. Each devout repetition of the Hail Mary commemorates and honors that ineffable mystery which was effected in the Blessed Virgin by the divine salutation, "Hail, full of grace," pronounced by the Archangel Gabriel when he greeted her on behalf of God and announced to her the coming and Incarnation of the Son of God, and her reception of the most lofty dignity of Mother of God.

Hence, you can not too often utter words so holy and so pleasing to the Son of God, so prized and honored by His glorious Mother, words which should be so cherished and highly revered among you. The Son of God delights in these words because He is well pleased that His most noble Mother should be hailed and honored, because all honor given to her returns again to Him and everything done for her is done for Him, even *more* than anything done for the least of His little ones. Then, too, these sacred words recall to mind the first mystery of His life, the mystery of His exceedingly great love for His Father and for us. They are most dear to and most honored by His Blessed Mother because they brought her the greatest and most sublime message of all time. These words should be highly valued and loved because they tell of the coming of One so eagerly awaited, so desired and prayed for on earth for five thousand years, the Redeemer descending to earth to deliver mankind from the tyranny of Satan and of sin, to reconcile man with God and to effect in each soul such great and marvelous things for love of men.

For these reasons the practice of reciting the Rosary, composed of repetitions of this holy and angelical salutation, is most holy, most pleasing to God and to the Mother of God, and it ought to be the customary practice of all true Christians.

I am very much afraid that those who shall be overtaken by death without this symbol, which is one of the characteristics of the servants and children of the Mother of God, may easily be disowned by her, and consequently rejected by her Son, as unworthy to share in the mercies of the Son or the favors of the Mother. But it is not enough simply to own and carry a rosary. The main thing is to say it well. And here is the way to do so.

A Devout Method of Reciting the Rosary

First kiss the cross of your rosary and make the *Sign of the Cross* with it in honor of and in union with the exceedingly great love of the Son of God when He kissed and took upon His shoulders the burden of the Cross. In doing this, **make an act of accepting and cherishing** all the crosses, trials and afflictions Jesus may send you in your whole life. Make this act in union with His love, which moved Him to make the same act. After that, say the *Credo* on the Cross.

In reciting the Creed, that apostolic summary of our faith, we must **give ourselves to Jesus** in union with the most burning love with which He died for us and with the love of all the holy martyrs who died for Him. We must do this, I repeat, in union with that same love, offer ourselves to Him to die and shed our blood a thousand times, were it possible, for His pure love, for the glory of His mysteries; martyrdom is to be preferred to the slightest deviation from the faith of His Church. So also, we must surrender ourselves to Him to be filled with a great love and devotion for all the mysteries of His life and of His Church, that He may implant and glorify them in us according to His holy will.

With the recitation of the *Our Father* and the three *Hail Marys* introducing the first decade, we should **renounce ourselves** at the feet of the Son of God and His holy Mother, considering ourselves most unworthy to appear before them or to think of them, or to have them think of us. And we should give ourselves to Jesus, imploring Him to reduce to nothing in us all which is opposed to Him, and to, take up His abode in us, that He Himself may honor His most blessed Mother on our behalf, for He alone can give her fitting honor. Each One of us must also **unite ourselves to His zeal, love and devotion** for her. Then we should offer our prayer to the Blessed Virgin, in union with the devotion, love, humility and purity of her Dear Son and in union with all the devout prayers and all the glory and praise, past, present and future, ever addressed to her Son and herself.

This should be offered for the accomplishment of their heavenly design, especially on behalf of ourselves.

After that, as each decade of the Rosary is said, we should offer it to the Son and the Mother, **in honor of one or another of their most eminent virtues**, never separating Jesus from Mary or Mary from Jesus. The offering of the decades proceeds as follows:

4

The first decade should be offered to Jesus and Mary in honor of the deep humility that characterized all their thoughts, words and actions.

The second decade should be said in honor of the perfect purity of the Heart of Jesus and Mary. This virtue consists chiefly of two elements, namely: first, a very great hatred, horror and flight from sin, together with perfect detachment from all that is not God; and second, a most holy union with God and the pure glory of God, which existed most eminently in the holy soul of the Son of God and that of His most holy Mother.

The third decade should be recited in honor of the divine meekness and charity which Jesus and Mary practiced towards others in their thoughts, words, actions and sufferings.

The fourth decade should be said in honor of the most holy obedience of Jesus and Mary to every operation of God's holy will. They never sought to do their own will, but rather chose the will of God in all and by all things, and the will of others for the love of God. What is more, they sought their entire satisfaction and joy in submitting to all that was willed by God and in fulfilling His every command or wish.

The fifth decade should be offered in honor of the boundless and ardent pure love of Jesus Christ for His Heavenly Father and of Mary for Jesus: for they both lived in an uninterrupted act of this pure love, and never had a thought or uttered a word or performed any action save in this pure love. It should also be said in honor of the last day, the last hour, the moment, and the death of Jesus and Mary – a death completely divine and all for love.

Now, as you say each decade:
1. You should meditate on each of these virtues of Jesus and Mary, considering their eminent sanctity, and with what perfection they practiced each virtue throughout their lifetime, in thought, word and action.
2. You should consider yourself and see how far removed you are from this virtue, and how little you resemble your Father and Mother (that is, Jesus and Mary) in this. Then, you should

profoundly humble yourself on this account and beg them to forgive you, to make reparation for your failures and to offer to the Eternal Father all the honor accorded Him by their practice of this virtue, in satisfaction for the faults you have committed against it.

3. Offer yourself to Jesus and to His holy Mother with an earnest resolution to attend with more care to the practice of this virtue in future, imploring the Divine Son, by His absolute power and the inviolate Mother by her prayers and merits, to destroy in your soul all that can possibly prevent you from making this progress, and to establish the reign of this virtue in you for His pure glory.

But please remember well what I have said elsewhere, that in all these devotions, even though I may suggest various ideas and practices to you, there is no need for you to make use of them all every time, but only of those from which you happen to derive the most spiritual benefit. Or else, use now one, now another, according to the inspiration of Our Lord's grace. For instance, if your mind finds enough to occupy it in contemplation of one or two of the virtues that have been mentioned, or in some other virtues of Jesus and Mary, there is no need to go on to the consideration of the others, which may be considered at another time.

It remains to be said that, when you recite the last decade in honor of the last hour and most holy death of Jesus and Mary, you should offer them the last moment of your life and the instant of your death, in honor of the last day, the last hour, and the last moment of their life, and their most holy death, imploring them to grant that all that shall occur in your last day and moment may be consecrated to the homage and the glory of what took place on their last day and at the moment of their death and that you may die in the state and practice of divine love, and that your last breath may be an act of most pure love for Jesus.

12 10 Hail Marys

11 Announce the
3rd Mystery
and Our Father

Glory Be 13

10 Glory Be

Announce the 14
4th Mystery
and Our Father

9 10 Hail Marys

10 Hail Marys 15

8 Announce the
2nd Mystery
and Our Father

7 Glory Be

Glory Be 16

Announce the 17
5th Mystery
and Our Father

6 10 Hail Marys

10 Hail Marys 18

Glory Be 19

5 Announce the
1st Mystery and
Our Father

Hail, Holy Queen 20

4 Glory Be

3 3 Hail Marys

Our Father

2 Our Father

Hail Marys

1 The Apostles' Creed

7

The Traditional Rosary Mysteries

The purpose of the Rosary is to help keep in memory certain principal events or mysteries in the history of our salvation, and to thank and praise God for them. There are fifteen mysteries traditionally reflected upon in the Rosary. Pope St. John Paul II added five mysteries he composed call the Luminous mysteries. Here, we present meditations on these twenty mysteries in the spirit of St. John Eudes.

Mysteries of Messianic Joy *(The Joyful Mysteries)*

1. **The Incarnation of the Son of God**

   We ask for the grace to be a continuation in ourselves of the incarnate presence of Jesus.

   LUKE 1:26-31 — In the sixth month, the angel Gabriel was sent from God to a town of Galilee called Nazareth, to a virgin betrothed to a man named Joseph, of the house of David, and the virgin's name was Mary. And coming to her, he said, "Hail, favored one! The Lord is with you." But she was greatly troubled at what was said and pondered what sort of greeting this might be. Then the angel said to her, "Do not be afraid, Mary, for you have found favor with God. Behold, you will conceive in your womb and bear a son, and you shall name him Jesus.

   MATTHEW 1:18-23 — Now this is how the birth of Jesus Christ came about. When his mother Mary was betrothed to Joseph, but before they lived together, she was found with child through the holy Spirit. Joseph her husband, since he was a righteous man, yet unwilling to expose her to shame, decided to divorce her quietly. Such was his intention when, behold, the angel of the Lord appeared to him in a dream and said, "Joseph, son of David, do not be afraid to take Mary your wife into your home. For it is through the holy Spirit that this child has been conceived in her. She will bear a son and you are to name him Jesus, because he will save his people from their sins." All this took place to fulfill what the Lord had said through the prophet: "Behold, the virgin shall be with child and bear a son, and they shall name him Emmanuel," which means "God is with us."

8

JOHN 1:9-14 — The true light, which enlightens everyone, was coming into the world. He was in the world, and the world came to be through him, but the world did not know him. He came to what was his own, but his own people did not accept him. But to those who did accept him he gave power to become children of God, to those who believe in his name, who were born not by natural generation nor by human choice nor by a man's decision but of God. And the Word became flesh and made his dwelling among us, and we saw his glory, the glory as of the Father's only Son, full of grace and truth.

2. **The Visit of Mary to St. Elizabeth**

   We ask Mary to always bring us to the presence of her Son Jesus, our Savior.

   LUKE 1:42-45 — cried out in a loud voice and said, "Most blessed are you among women, and blessed is the fruit of your womb. And how does this happen to me, that the mother of my Lord should come to me? For at the moment the sound of your greeting reached my ears, the infant in my womb leaped for joy. Blessed are you who believed that what was spoken to you by the Lord would be fulfilled."

   LUKE 1:51-55 — He has shown might with his arm, dispersed the arrogant of mind and heart. He has thrown down the rulers from their thrones but lifted up the lowly. The hungry he has filled with good things; the rich he has sent away empty. He has helped Israel his servant, remembering his mercy, according to his promise to our fathers, to Abraham and to his descendants forever."

   REVELATION 3:19-20 — Those whom I love, I reprove and chastise. Be earnest, therefore, and repent. Behold, I stand at the door and knock. If anyone hears my voice and opens the door, [then] I will enter his house and dine with him, and he with me.

3. **The Birth of Our Lord Jesus Christ**

   With Mary, Joseph, and the shepherds, let us receive our Savior and place all our hope in Him.

   LUKE 2:4-7 — And Joseph too went up from Galilee from the town of Nazareth to Judea, to the city of David that is called Bethlehem, because he was of the house and family of David, to be enrolled with Mary, his betrothed, who was with child. While they were there, the time came for her to have her child, and she gave birth to her firstborn son. She wrapped him in swaddling clothes and laid him in a manger, because there was no room for them in the inn.

GALATIANS 4:4-7 — But when the fullness of time had come, God sent his Son, born of a woman, born under the law, to ransom those under the law, so that we might receive adoption. As proof that you are children, God sent the spirit of his Son into our hearts, crying out, "Abba, Father!" So you are no longer a slave but a child, and if a child then also an heir, through God.

4. The Presentation of Jesus in the Temple

With Jesus, let us present ourselves to the Father so that in us, He may be light to the world.

LUKE 2:22-24 — When the days were completed for their purification according to the law of Moses, they took him up to Jerusalem to present him to the Lord, just as it is written in the law of the Lord, "Every male that opens the womb shall be consecrated to the Lord," and to offer the sacrifice of "a pair of turtledoves or two young pigeons," in accordance with the dictate in the law of the Lord.

LUKE 2:25-32 — Now there was a man in Jerusalem whose name was Simeon. This man was righteous and devout, awaiting the consolation of Israel, and the holy Spirit was upon him. It had been revealed to him by the holy Spirit that he should not see death before he had seen the Messiah of the Lord. He came in the Spirit into the temple; and when the parents brought in the child Jesus to perform the custom of the law in regard to him, he took him into his arms and blessed God, saying: "Now, Master, you may let your servant go in peace, according to your word, for my eyes have seen your salvation, which you prepared in sight of all the peoples, a light for revelation to the Gentiles, and glory for your people Israel."

MATTHEW 3:1-4 — In those days John the Baptist appeared, preaching in the desert of Judea [and] saying, "Repent, for the kingdom of heaven is at hand!" It was of him that the prophet Isaiah had spoken when he said: "A voice of one crying out in the desert, 'Prepare the way of the Lord, make straight his paths.'" John wore clothing made of camel's hair and had a leather belt around his waist. His food was locusts and wild honey.

5. **The Loss and Finding of Jesus in the Temple**

    With Jesus, let us tell our Father that we are ready to take up our part in the plan of salvation.

    LUKE 2:42-47 — When he was twelve years old, they went up according to festival custom. After they had completed its days, as they were returning, the boy Jesus remained behind in Jerusalem, but his parents did not know it. Thinking that he was in the caravan, they journeyed for a day and looked for him among their relatives and acquaintances, but not finding him, they returned to Jerusalem to look for him. After three days they found him in the temple, sitting in the midst of the teachers, listening to them and asking them questions, and all who heard him were astounded at his understanding and his answers.

    LUKE 2:46-50 — After three days they found him in the temple, sitting in the midst of the teachers, listening to them and asking them questions, and all who heard him were astounded at his understanding and his answers. When his parents saw him, they were astonished, and his mother said to him, "Son, why have you done this to us? Your father and I have been looking for you with great anxiety." And he said to them, "Why were you looking for me? Did you not know that I must be in my Father's house?" But they did not understand what he said to them.

    PSALMS 24:1-6 — A psalm of David. The earth is the Lord's and all it holds, the world and those who dwell in it. For he founded it on the seas, established it over the rivers. Who may go up the mountain of the Lord? Who can stand in his holy place? "The clean of hand and pure of heart, who has not given his soul to useless things, what is vain. He will receive blessings from the Lord, and justice from his saving God. Such is the generation that seeks him, that seeks the face of the God of Jacob."

Mysteries of the Saving Passion
(The Sorrowful Mysteries)

1. Jesus' Prayer in the Garden

Let us say with Jesus: "not my will, Father, but Yours be done."

LUKE 22:39-43 — Then going out he went, as was his custom, to the Mount of Olives, and the disciples followed him. When he arrived at the place he said to them, "Pray that you may not undergo the test." After withdrawing about a stone's throw from them and kneeling, he prayed, saying, "Father, if you are willing, take this cup away from me; still, not my will but yours be done." And to strengthen him an angel from heaven appeared to him.

ISAIAH 53:1-3 — Who would believe what we have heard? To whom has the arm of the Lord been revealed? He grew up like a sapling before him, like a shoot from the parched earth; He had no majestic bearing to catch our eye, no beauty to draw us to him. He was spurned and avoided by men, a man of suffering, knowing pain, Like one from whom you turn your face, spurned, and we held him in no esteem.

HEBREWS 5:5-10 — In the same way, it was not Christ who glorified himself in becoming high priest, but rather the one who said to him: "You are my son; this day I have begotten you"; just as he says in another place: "You are a priest forever according to the order of Melchizedek." In the days when he was in the flesh, he offered prayers and supplications with loud cries and tears to the one who was able to save him from death, and he was heard because of his reverence. Son though he was, he learned obedience from what he suffered; and when he was made perfect, he became the source of eternal salvation for all who obey him, declared by God high priest according to the order of Melchizedek.

2. The Scourging of Our Lord

Let us say with St. Paul: "I complete in myself what is lacking in the passion of our Lord."

MARK 15:16-20 — The soldiers led him away inside the palace, that is, the praetorium, and assembled the whole cohort. They clothed him in purple and, weaving a crown of thorns, placed it on him. They began to salute him with, "Hail, King of the Jews!" and kept striking his head with a reed and spitting upon him. They knelt before him in homage. And when they had mocked him, they stripped him of the purple cloak, dressed him in his own clothes, and led him out to crucify him.

12

ISAIAH 53:4-5 — Yet it was our pain that he bore, our sufferings he endured. We thought of him as stricken, struck down by God and afflicted, But he was pierced for our sins, crushed for our iniquity. He bore the punishment that makes us whole, by his wounds we were healed.

COLOSSIANS 1:24 — Now I rejoice in my sufferings for your sake, and in my flesh I am filling up what is lacking in the afflictions of Christ on behalf of his body, which is the church,

3. **The Crowning with Thorns**

Let us adore Jesus as our King and Savior.

JOHN 19:1-3 — Then Pilate took Jesus and had him scourged. And the soldiers wove a crown out of thorns and placed it on his head, and clothed him in a purple cloak, and they came to him and said, "Hail, King of the Jews!" And they struck him repeatedly.

GALATIANS 2:19-20 — For through the law I died to the law, that I might live for God. I have been crucified with Christ; yet I live, no longer I, but Christ lives in me; insofar as I now live in the flesh, I live by faith in the Son of God who has loved me and given himself up for me.

LUKE 22:63-65 — The men who held Jesus in custody were ridiculing and beating him. They blindfolded him and questioned him, saying, "Prophesy! Who is it that struck you?" And they reviled him in saying many other things against him.

4. **Jesus Carries the Cross on His Shoulders**

Let us resolve to carry the crosses of life and follow in the footsteps of Jesus.

LUKE 23:26-28 — As they led him away they took hold of a certain Simon, a Cyrenian, who was coming in from the country; and after laying the cross on him, they made him carry it behind Jesus. A large crowd of people followed Jesus, including many women who mourned and lamented him. Jesus turned to them and said, "Daughters of Jerusalem, do not weep for me; weep instead for yourselves and for your children,

LUKE 14:23-27 — The master then ordered the servant, 'Go out to the highways and hedgerows and make people come in that my home may be filled. For, I tell you, none of those men who were invited will taste my dinner.'" Great crowds were traveling with him, and he turned and addressed them, "If any one comes to me without hating his father and mother, wife and children, brothers and sisters, and even his own life, he cannot be my disciple. Whoever does not carry his own cross and come after me cannot be my disciple.

HEBREWS 13:12-13 — Therefore, Jesus also suffered outside the gate, to consecrate the people by his own blood. Let us then go to him outside the camp, bearing the reproach that he bore.

5. The Crucifixion and Death of Our Lord Jesus

Oh Christ, grant that we may live with You, die with You, and rise with You.

JOHN 19:28-30 — After this, aware that everything was now finished, in order that the scripture might be fulfilled, Jesus said, "I thirst." There was a vessel filled with common wine. So they put a sponge soaked in wine on a sprig of hyssop and put it up to his mouth. When Jesus had taken the wine, he said, "It is finished." And bowing his head, he handed over the spirit.

GALATIANS 6:14 — But may I never boast except in the cross of our Lord Jesus Christ, through which the world has been crucified to me, and I to the world.

Mysteries of the Glory of God
(The Glorious Mysteries)

1. **The Resurrection of Our Lord**

   Lord Jesus, bring us to resurrection through the grace of our baptism.

   LUKE 24:1-6 — But at daybreak on the first day of the week they took the spices they had prepared and went to the tomb. They found the stone rolled away from the tomb; but when they entered, they did not find the body of the Lord Jesus. While they were puzzling over this, behold, two men in dazzling garments appeared to them. They were terrified and bowed their faces to the ground. They said to them, "Why do you seek the living one among the dead? He is not here, but he has been raised. Remember what he said to you while he was still in Galilee,

   ROMANS 6:1-4 — What then shall we say? Shall we persist in sin that grace may abound? Of course not! How can we who died to sin yet live in it? Or are you unaware that we who were baptized into Christ Jesus were baptized into his death? We were indeed buried with him through baptism into death, so that, just as Christ was raised from the dead by the glory of the Father, we too might live in newness of life.

   COLOSSIANS 3:1-4 — If then you were raised with Christ, seek what is above, where Christ is seated at the right hand of God. Think of what is above, not of what is on earth. For you have died, and your life is hidden with Christ in God. When Christ your life appears, then you too will appear with him in glory.

2. **The Ascension of Our Lord Jesus**

   Lord Jesus, bring us with You, one day, to our heavenly Father.

   LUKE 24:50-53 — Then he led them [out] as far as Bethany, raised his hands, and blessed them. As he blessed them he parted from them and was taken up to heaven. They did him homage and then returned to Jerusalem with great joy, and they were continually in the temple praising God.

   EPHESIANS 4:7-10 — But grace was given to each of us according to the measure of Christ's gift. Therefore, it says: "He ascended on high and took prisoners captive; he gave gifts to men." What does "he ascended" mean except that he also descended into the lower [regions] of the earth? The one who descended is also the one who ascended far above all the heavens, that he might fill all things.

HEBREWS 9:11-12 — But when Christ came as high priest of the good things that have come to be, passing through the greater and more perfect tabernacle not made by hands, that is, not belonging to this creation, he entered once for all into the sanctuary, not with the blood of goats and calves but with his own blood, thus obtaining eternal redemption.

3. **The Coming of the Holy Spirit to the Church**

Spirit of God, fill us with Your gifts and with Your fruits.

ACTS 2:1-4 — When the time for Pentecost was fulfilled, they were all in one place together. And suddenly there came from the sky a noise like a strong driving wind, and it filled the entire house in which they were. Then there appeared to them tongues as of fire, which parted and came to rest on each one of them. And they were all filled with the holy Spirit and began to speak in different tongues, as the Spirit enabled them to proclaim.

GALATIANS 5:22-24 — In contrast, the fruit of the Spirit is love, joy, peace, patience, kindness, generosity, faithfulness, gentleness, self-control. Against such there is no law. Now those who belong to Christ [Jesus] have crucified their flesh with its passions and desires.

4. **The Assumption of the Virgin Mary into Glory**

Lord Jesus, bring us, with Mary, into the fullness of Your glory.

1 CORINTHIANS 15:54-57 — And when this which is corruptible clothes itself with incorruptibility and this which is mortal clothes itself with immortality, then the word that is written shall come about: "Death is swallowed up in victory. Where, O death, is your victory? Where, O death, is your sting?" The sting of death is sin, and the power of sin is the law. But thanks be to God who gives us the victory through our Lord Jesus Christ.

GENESIS 3:14-15 — Then the Lord God said to the snake: Because you have done this, cursed are you among all the animals, tame or wild; On your belly you shall crawl, and dust you shall eat all the days of your life. I will put enmity between you and the woman, and between your offspring and hers; They will strike at your head, while you strike at their heel.

5. **The Coronation of Mary in Heaven**

Lord Jesus, grant us the motherly protection of the Virgin Mary.

REVELATION 12:1-2 — A great sign appeared in the sky, a woman clothed with the sun, with the moon under her feet, and on her head a crown of twelve stars. She was with child and wailed aloud in pain as she labored to give birth.

REVELATION 12: 5-6 — She gave birth to a son, a male child, destined to rule all the nations with an iron rod. Her child was caught up to God and his throne. The woman herself fled into the desert where she had a place prepared by God, that there she might be taken care of for twelve hundred and sixty days.

REVELATION 22:1-5 — Then the angel showed me the river of life-giving water, sparkling like crystal, flowing from the throne of God and of the Lamb down the middle of its street. On either side of the river grew the tree of life that produces fruit twelve times a year, once each month; the leaves of the trees serve as medicine for the nations. Nothing accursed will be found there anymore. The throne of God and of the Lamb will be in it, and his servants will worship him. They will look upon his face, and his name will be on their foreheads. Night will be no more, nor will they need light from lamp or sun, for the Lord God shall give them light, and they shall reign forever and ever.

ROMANS 8:37-39 — No, in all these things we conquer overwhelmingly through him who loved us. For I am convinced that neither death, nor life, nor angels, nor principalities, nor present things, nor future things, nor powers, nor height, nor depth, nor any other creature will be able to separate us from the love of God in Christ Jesus our Lord.

Mysteries of Divine Light

The following section is a composition of Fr. Alvaro Torres CJM

1. The Baptism of Our Lord Jesus

Lord, baptize us with water and with the fire of the Holy Spirit.

MATTHEW 3:13-17 — Then Jesus came from Galilee to John at the Jordan to be baptized by him. John tried to prevent him, saying, "I need to be baptized by you, and yet you are coming to me?" Jesus said to him in reply, "Allow it now, for thus it is fitting for us to fulfill all righteousness." Then he allowed him. After Jesus was baptized, he came up from the water and behold, the heavens were opened [for him], and he saw the Spirit of God descending like a dove [and] coming upon him. And a voice came from the heavens, saying, "This is my beloved Son, with whom I am well pleased."

JOHN 1:26-31 — John answered them, "I baptize with water; but there is one among you whom you do not recognize, the one who is coming after me, whose sandal strap I am not worthy to untie." This happened in Bethany across the Jordan, where John was baptizing. John the Baptist's Testimony to Jesus. The next day he saw Jesus coming toward him and said, "Behold, the Lamb of God, who takes away the sin of the world. He is the one of whom I said, 'A man is coming after me who ranks ahead of me because he existed before me.' I did not know him, but the reason why I came baptizing with water was that he might be made known to Israel."

2. Jesus and Mary in the Wedding at Cana

Lord Jesus, receive us into the eternal wedding feast of the Lamb.

JOHN 2:1-12 — On the third day there was a wedding in Cana in Galilee, and the mother of Jesus was there. Jesus and his disciples were also invited to the wedding. When the wine ran short, the mother of Jesus said to him, "They have no wine." [And] Jesus said to her, "Woman, how does your concern affect me? My hour has not yet come." His mother said to the servers, "Do whatever he tells you." Now there were six stone water jars there for Jewish ceremonial washings, each holding twenty to thirty gallons. Jesus told them, "Fill the jars with water." So they filled them to the brim. Then he told them, "Draw some out now and take it to the headwaiter." So they took it. And when the headwaiter tasted the water that had become wine, without knowing where it came from (although the servers who had drawn the water knew), the headwaiter called the bridegroom and said to him, "Everyone serves good wine first, and then when people have drunk freely, an inferior one; but you have kept the good wine until now." Jesus did this as the beginning of his signs in Cana in Galilee and so revealed his glory, and his disciples began to believe in him. After this, he and his mother, [his] brothers, and his disciples went down to Capernaum and stayed there only a few days.

ISAIAH 25:6 — On this mountain the Lord of hosts will provide for all peoples. A feast of rich food and choice wines, juicy, rich food and pure, choice wines.

REVELATION 19:9 — Then the angel said to me, "Write this: Blessed are those who have been called to the wedding feast of the Lamb." And he said to me, "These words are true; they come from God."

3. **Jesus Announces the Coming of the Kingdom of God**
Lord Jesus, grant that the saving action of Your kingdom comes to us.

MARK 1:14-15 — After John had been arrested, Jesus came to Galilee proclaiming the gospel of God: "This is the time of fulfillment. The kingdom of God is at hand. Repent, and believe in the gospel."

MATTHEW 11:2-6 — When John heard in prison of the works of the Messiah, he sent his disciples to him with this question, "Are you the one who is to come, or should we look for another?" Jesus said to them in reply, "Go and tell John what you hear and see: the blind regain their sight, the lame walk, lepers are cleansed, the deaf hear, the dead are raised, and the poor have the good news proclaimed to them. And blessed is the one who takes no offense at me."

4. **The Transfiguration of Our Lord**
Lord Jesus, transfigure us in Your image.

LUKE 9:28-36 — About eight days after he said this, he took Peter, John, and James and went up the mountain to pray. While he was praying his face changed in appearance and his clothing became dazzling white. And behold, two men were conversing with him, Moses and Elijah, who appeared in glory and spoke of his exodus that he was going to accomplish in Jerusalem. Peter and his companions had been overcome by sleep, but becoming fully awake, they saw his glory and the two men standing with him. As they were about to part from him, Peter said to Jesus, "Master, it is good that we are here; let us make three tents, one for you, one for Moses, and one for Elijah." But he did not know what he was saying. While he was still speaking, a cloud came and cast a shadow over them, and they became frightened when they entered the cloud. Then from the cloud came a voice that said, "This is my chosen Son; listen to him." After the voice had spoken, Jesus was found alone. They fell silent and did not at that time tell anyone what they had seen.

2 PETER 1:16-18 — We did not follow cleverly devised myths when we made known to you the power and coming of our Lord Jesus Christ, but we had been eyewitnesses of his majesty. For he received honor and glory from God the Father when that unique declaration came to him from the majestic glory, "This is my Son, my beloved, with whom I am well pleased." We ourselves heard this voice come from heaven while we were with him on the holy mountain.

2 CORINTHIANS 3:18 — All of us, gazing with unveiled face on the glory of the Lord, are being transformed into the same image from glory to glory, as from the Lord who is the Spirit.

5. **The Eucharist, Living Presence of Our Lord Jesus**

Lord Jesus, nourish us always with this bread for our journey into glory.

JOHN 6:51-59 — I am the living bread that came down from heaven; whoever eats this bread will live forever; and the bread that I will give is my flesh for the life of the world." The Jews quarreled among themselves, saying, "How can this man give us [his] flesh to eat?" Jesus said to them, "Amen, amen, I say to you, unless you eat the flesh of the Son of Man and drink his blood, you do not have life within you. Whoever eats my flesh and drinks my blood has eternal life, and I will raise him on the last day. For my flesh is true food, and my blood is true drink. Whoever eats my flesh and drinks my blood remains in me and I in him. Just as the living Father sent me and I have life because of the Father, so also the one who feeds on me will have life because of me. This is the bread that came down from heaven. Unlike your ancestors who ate and still died, whoever eats this bread will live forever." These things he said while teaching in the synagogue in Capernaum.

LUKE 22:14-19 — When the hour came, he took his place at table with the apostles. He said to them, "I have eagerly desired to eat this Passover with you before I suffer, for, I tell you, I shall not eat it [again] until there is fulfillment in the kingdom of God." Then he took a cup, gave thanks, and said, "Take this and share it among yourselves; for I tell you [that] from this time on I shall not drink of the fruit of the vine until the kingdom of God comes." Then he took the bread, said the blessing, broke it, and gave it to them, saying, "This is my body, which will be given for you; do this in memory of me."

Mysteries of the Rosary for the Liturgical Year

The following section is a composition of Fr. Alvaro Torres CJM

Here, we suggest a way of praying the Rosary along with the liturgical seasons.

It is recommended that popular devotions, as much as possible, are used in harmony with the liturgy. This enriches our experience of both, and keeps us from praying without paying attention to the liturgical seasons given to us by the Church.

Advent Mysteries

1. **The Divine Promise of a Messiah and Savior**

   With the desire of the holy ones in the first covenant, let us hope for the Messiah

   LUKE 2:25 — Now there was a man in Jerusalem whose name was Simeon. This man was righteous and devout, awaiting the consolation of Israel, and the holy Spirit was upon him.

   LUKE 2:36 — There was also a prophetess, Anna, the daughter of Phanuel, of the tribe of Asher. She was advanced in years, having lived seven years with her husband after her marriage,

   LUKE 2:38 — And coming forward at that very time, she gave thanks to God and spoke about the child to all who were awaiting the redemption of Jerusalem.

   ISAIAH 45:8 — Let justice descend, you heavens, like dew from above, like gentle rain let the clouds drop it down. Let the earth open and salvation bud forth; let righteousness spring up with them! I, the Lord, have created this.

2. **The Wedding of Mary and Joseph**

    God our Father, You are at work preparing a home in the world for Your Son, Jesus.

    LUKE 1:26-27 — In the sixth month, the angel Gabriel was sent from God to a town of Galilee called Nazareth, to a virgin betrothed to a man named Joseph, of the house of David, and the virgin's name was Mary.

    LUKE 2:4-5 — And Joseph too went up from Galilee from the town of Nazareth to Judea, to the city of David that is called Bethlehem, because he was of the house and family of David, to be enrolled with Mary, his betrothed, who was with child.

    MATTHEW 1:18 — Now this is how the birth of Jesus Christ came about. When his mother Mary was betrothed to Joseph, but before they lived together, she was found with child through the holy Spirit.

3. **Mary Waits for the Promised Birth of her Son, Jesus Christ**

    Together with Mary, let us wait with love for the coming of Jesus, our Lord.

    LUKE 1:38 — Mary said, "Behold, I am the handmaid of the Lord. May it be done to me according to your word." Then the angel departed from her.

    LUKE 2:4-5 — And Joseph too went up from Galilee from the town of Nazareth to Judea, to the city of David that is called Bethlehem, because he was of the house and family of David, to be enrolled with Mary, his betrothed, who was with child.

4. **God Entrusts St. Joseph with the Care of His Son, Jesus.**

    With Joseph, let us accept the mystery of the virgin birth of the Messiah.

    MATTHEW 1:19-21 — Joseph her husband, since he was a righteous man, yet unwilling to expose her to shame, decided to divorce her quietly. Such was his intention when, behold, the angel of the Lord appeared to him in a dream and said, "Joseph, son of David, do not be afraid to take Mary your wife into your home. For it is through the holy Spirit that this child has been conceived in her. She will bear a son and you are to name him Jesus, because he will save his people from their sins."

5. **The Glorious Coming of the Lord at the End of Time**

   With the first Christians, let us acclaim: Maranatha, come Lord Jesus!

   MARK 14:61-62 — But he was silent and answered nothing. Again the high priest asked him and said to him, "Are you the Messiah, the son of the Blessed One?" Then Jesus answered, "I am; and 'you will see the Son of Man seated at the right hand of the Power and coming with the clouds of heaven.'"

   REVELATION 1:7 — Behold, he is coming amid the clouds, and every eye will see him, even those who pierced him. All the peoples of the earth will lament him. Yes. Amen.

Advent – O Antiphons

Another Advent option, inspired by the "O" antiphons from the office of vespers leading up to Christmas.

[The hymn *Oh Come, Oh Come, Emmanuel* may be sung between mysteries.]

1. **Jesus, eternal Wisdom,**
   come and fill the Church with divine wisdom.

2. **Jesus, Lord and King, hoped for by all mankind,**
   come in Your power to save our humanity.

3. **Jesus, Key of David,**
   come and open to all the gates of Your kingdom.

4. **Jesus, Morning Star,**
   come bring light and warmth to Your
   Church and to the world.

5. **Jesus, Emmanuel, God with us,**
   come and dwell in our home on earth.

Christmas Mysteries

1. The Father Announces to us the Temporal Birth of His Son

Let us ask for peace and salvation to come into our world.

LUKE 2:9-11 — The angel of the Lord appeared to them and the glory of the Lord shone around them, and they were struck with great fear. The angel said to them, "Do not be afraid; for behold, I proclaim to you good news of great joy that will be for all the people. For today in the city of David a savior has been born for you who is Messiah and Lord.

2. Mary and Joseph Receive Jesus, the Messiah

With Mary and Joseph, let us lovingly receive the Emmanuel, God with us.

LUKE 2:6-7 — While they were there, the time came for her to have her child, and she gave birth to her firstborn son. She wrapped him in swaddling clothes and laid him in a manger, because there was no room for them in the inn.

MATTHEW 1:24-25 — When Joseph awoke, he did as the angel of the Lord had commanded him and took his wife into his home. He had no relations with her until she bore a son, and he named him Jesus.

3. The Shepherds Seek and Find Jesus, the Savior

We, the poor of the world, let us go meet the Savior.

LUKE 2:15-17 — When the angels went away from them to heaven, the shepherds said to one another, "Let us go, then, to Bethlehem to see this thing that has taken place, which the Lord has made known to us." So they went in haste and found Mary and Joseph, and the infant lying in the manger. When they saw this, they made known the message that had been told them about this child.

4. **The Magi Come From Afar to Seek the Savior**

Let us pray that all the people of the world come to know Jesus, the Savior.

MATTHEW 2:1-2 — When Jesus was born in Bethlehem of Judea, in the days of King Herod, behold, magi from the east arrived in Jerusalem, saying, "Where is the newborn king of the Jews? We saw his star at its rising and have come to do him homage."

MATTHEW 2:11-12 — and on entering the house they saw the child with Mary his mother. They prostrated themselves and did him homage. Then they opened their treasures and offered him gifts of gold, frankincense, and myrrh. And having been warned in a dream not to return to Herod, they departed for their country by another way.

5. **The Life of the Holy Family: Jesus, Mary and Joseph**

Let us imitate, in our own families and communities, the life of this holy Family.

LUKE 2:51-52 — He went down with them and came to Nazareth, and was obedient to them; and his mother kept all these things in her heart. And Jesus advanced [in] wisdom and age and favor before God and man.

Lenten Mysteries

1. Jesus is Tempted in the Desert

Let us cling to the will of the Father through all temptation.

MATTHEW 4:1-11 — Then Jesus was led by the Spirit into the desert to be tempted by the devil. He fasted for forty days and forty nights, and afterwards he was hungry. The tempter approached and said to him, "If you are the Son of God, command that these stones become loaves of bread." He said in reply, "It is written: 'One does not live by bread alone, but by every word that comes forth from the mouth of God.'" Then the devil took him to the holy city, and made him stand on the parapet of the temple, and said to him, "If you are the Son of God, throw yourself down. For it is written: 'He will command his angels concerning you' and 'with their hands they will support you, lest you dash your foot against a stone.'" Jesus answered him, "Again it is written, 'You shall not put the Lord, your God, to the test.'" Then the devil took him up to a very high mountain, and showed him all the kingdoms of the world in their magnificence, and he said to him, "All these I shall give to you, if you will prostrate yourself and worship me." At this, Jesus said to him, "Get away, Satan! It is written: 'The Lord, your God, shall you worship and him alone shall you serve.'" Then the devil left him and, behold, angels came and ministered to him.

LUKE 4:1-13 — Filled with the holy Spirit, Jesus returned from the Jordan and was led by the Spirit into the desert for forty days, to be tempted by the devil. He ate nothing during those days, and when they were over he was hungry. The devil said to him, "If you are the Son of God, command this stone to become bread." Jesus answered him, "It is written, 'One does not live by bread alone.'" Then he took him up and showed him all the kingdoms of the world in a single instant. The devil said to him, "I shall give to you all this power and their glory; for it has been handed over to me, and I may give it to whomever I wish. All this will be yours, if you worship me." Jesus said to him in reply, "It is written: 'You shall worship the Lord, your God, and him alone shall you serve.'" Then he led him to Jerusalem, made him stand on the parapet of the temple, and said to him, "If you are the Son of God, throw yourself down from here, for it is written: 'He will command his angels concerning you, to guard you,' and: 'With their hands they will support you, lest you dash your foot against a stone.'" Jesus said to him in reply, "It also says, 'You shall not put the Lord, your God, to the test.'" When the devil had finished every temptation, he departed from him for a time.

2. **Jesus, Lamb of God who Takes Away the Sins of the World**

   Through Your passion, Lord, purify us from all our sins.

   JOHN 1:29 — The next day he saw Jesus coming toward him and said, "Behold, the Lamb of God, who takes away the sin of the world.

3. **Jesus Calls us to Conversion**

   Grant, oh Lord, that we may definitively abandon our evil ways.

   MARK 1:14-15 — After John had been arrested, Jesus came to Galilee proclaiming the gospel of God: "This is the time of fulfillment. The kingdom of God is at hand. Repent, and believe in the gospel."

   LUKE 13:2-5 — He said to them in reply, "Do you think that because these Galileans suffered in this way they were greater sinners than all other Galileans? By no means! But I tell you, if you do not repent, you will all perish as they did! Or those eighteen people who were killed when the tower at Siloam fell on them]—do you think they were more guilty than everyone else who lived in Jerusalem? By no means! But I tell you, if you do not repent, you will all perish as they did!"

4. **Jesus Asks Us to Believe in Him and in the Gospel**

   May the Lord grant us the gift of faith.

   JOHN 14:1 — Do not let your hearts be troubled. You have faith in God; have faith also in me.

   MARK 1:13 — and he remained in the desert for forty days, tempted by Satan. He was among wild beasts, and the angels ministered to him.

   MARK 8:35 — For whoever wishes to save his life will lose it, but whoever loses his life for my sake and that of the gospel will save it.

5. **The Lord has Baptized us with Fire and the Holy Spirit**

   Let us renew our commitments and baptismal promises.

   LUKE 3:16 — John answered them all, saying, "I am baptizing you with water, but one mightier than I is coming. I am not worthy to loosen the thongs of his sandals. He will baptize you with the holy Spirit and fire.

Holy Week Mysteries

1. The Messianic Entry of Jesus into Jerusalem

As the poor of the world, today we cry out: "Hosanna! Save us, oh Lord."

MARK 11:1-11 — When they drew near to Jerusalem, to Bethphage and Bethany at the Mount of Olives, he sent two of his disciples and said to them, "Go into the village opposite you, and immediately on entering it, you will find a colt tethered on which no one has ever sat. Untie it and bring it here. If anyone should say to you, 'Why are you doing this?' reply, 'The Master has need of it and will send it back here at once.'" So they went off and found a colt tethered at a gate outside on the street, and they untied it. Some of the bystanders said to them, "What are you doing, untying the colt?" They answered them just as Jesus had told them to, and they permitted them to do it. So they brought the colt to Jesus and put their cloaks over it. And he sat on it. Many people spread their cloaks on the road, and others spread leafy branches that they had cut from the fields. Those preceding him as well as those following kept crying out: "Hosanna! Blessed is he who comes in the name of the Lord! Blessed is the kingdom of our father David that is to come! Hosanna in the highest!" He entered Jerusalem and went into the temple area. He looked around at everything and, since it was already late, went out to Bethany with the Twelve.

JOHN 12:12-19 — On the next day, when the great crowd that had come to the feast heard that Jesus was coming to Jerusalem, they took palm branches and went out to meet him, and cried out: "Hosanna! Blessed is he who comes in the name of the Lord, [even] the king of Israel." Jesus found an ass and sat upon it, as is written: "Fear no more, O daughter Zion; see, your king comes, seated upon an ass's colt." His disciples did not understand this at first, but when Jesus had been glorified they remembered that these things were written about him and that they had done this for him. So the crowd that was with him when he called Lazarus from the tomb and raised him from death continued to testify. This was [also] why the crowd went to meet him, because they heard that he had done this sign. So the Pharisees said to one another, "You see that you are gaining nothing. Look, the whole world has gone after him."

2. **The Anointing in Bethany**

We prepare ourselves with You, Lord, for Your death and burial.

JOHN 12:1-8 — Six days before Passover Jesus came to Bethany, where Lazarus was, whom Jesus had raised from the dead. They gave a dinner for him there, and Martha served, while Lazarus was one of those reclining at table with him. Mary took a liter of costly perfumed oil made from genuine aromatic nard and anointed the feet of Jesus and dried them with her hair; the house was filled with the fragrance of the oil. Then Judas the Iscariot, one [of] his disciples, and the one who would betray him, said, "Why was this oil not sold for three hundred days' wages and given to the poor?" He said this not because he cared about the poor but because he was a thief and held the money bag and used to steal the contributions. So Jesus said, "Leave her alone. Let her keep this for the day of my burial. You always have the poor with you, but you do not always have me."

MATTHEW 26:6-13 — Now when Jesus was in Bethany in the house of Simon the leper, a woman came up to him with an alabaster jar of costly perfumed oil, and poured it on his head while he was reclining at table. When the disciples saw this, they were indignant and said, "Why this waste? It could have been sold for much, and the money given to the poor." Since Jesus knew this, he said to them, "Why do you make trouble for the woman? She has done a good thing for me. The poor you will always have with you; but you will not always have me. In pouring this perfumed oil upon my body, she did it to prepare me for burial. Amen, I say to you, wherever this gospel is proclaimed in the whole world, what she has done will be spoken of, in memory of her."

3. **The Pascal Feast of the New Covenant**

Lord, may we always joyfully celebrate Your Eucharist.

LUKE 22:14-23 — When the hour came, he took his place at table with the apostles. He said to them, "I have eagerly desired to eat this Passover with you before I suffer, for, I tell you, I shall not eat it [again] until there is fulfillment in the kingdom of God." Then he took a cup, gave thanks, and said, "Take this and share it among yourselves; for I tell you [that] from this time on I shall not drink of the fruit of the vine until the kingdom of God comes." Then he took the bread, said the blessing, broke it, and gave it to them, saying, "This is my body, which will be given for you; do this in memory of me." And likewise the cup after they had eaten, saying, "This cup is the new covenant in my blood, which will be shed for you.

MARK 14:22-26 — While they were eating, he took bread, said the blessing, broke it, and gave it to them, and said, "Take it; this is my body." Then he took a cup, gave thanks, and gave it to them, and they all drank from it. He said to them, "This is my blood of the covenant, which will be shed for many. Amen, I say to you, I shall not drink again the fruit of the vine until the day when I drink it new in the kingdom of God." Then, after singing a hymn, they went out to the Mount of Olives.

4.   **The Crucifixion and Death of Jesus, the Son of God**

I am crucified with Christ; He lives in me! (Galatians 2:19-20).

JOHN 19:18-30 — There they crucified him, and with him two others, one on either side, with Jesus in the middle. Pilate also had an inscription written and put on the cross. It read, "Jesus the Nazorean, the King of the Jews." Now many of the Jews read this inscription, because the place where Jesus was crucified was near the city; and it was written in Hebrew, Latin, and Greek. So the chief priests of the Jews said to Pilate, "Do not write 'The King of the Jews,' but that he said, 'I am the King of the Jews.'" Pilate answered, "What I have written, I have written." When the soldiers had crucified Jesus, they took his clothes and divided them into four shares, a share for each soldier. They also took his tunic, but the tunic was seamless, woven in one piece from the top down. So they said to one another, "Let's not tear it, but cast lots for it to see whose it will be," in order that the passage of scripture might be fulfilled [that says]: "They divided my garments among them, and for my vesture they cast lots." This is what the soldiers did. Standing by the cross of Jesus were his mother and his mother's sister, Mary the wife of Clopas, and Mary of Magdala. When Jesus saw his mother and the disciple there whom he loved, he said to his mother, "Woman, behold, your son." Then he said to the disciple, "Behold, your mother." And from that hour the disciple took her into his home. After this, aware that everything was now finished, in order that the scripture might be fulfilled, Jesus said, "I thirst." There was a vessel filled with common wine. So they put a sponge soaked in wine on a sprig of hyssop and put it up to his mouth. When Jesus had taken the wine, he said, "It is finished." And bowing his head, he handed over the spirit.

5. **The Burial of Jesus, Messiah and Lord**

In baptism, we have been buried with Christ (Romans 6:4).

JOHN 19:38-42 — After this, Joseph of Arimathea, secretly a disciple of Jesus for fear of the Jews, asked Pilate if he could remove the body of Jesus. And Pilate permitted it. So he came and took his body. Nicodemus, the one who had first come to him at night, also came bringing a mixture of myrrh and aloes weighing about one hundred pounds. They took the body of Jesus and bound it with burial cloths along with the spices, according to the Jewish burial custom. Now in the place where he had been crucified there was a garden, and in the garden a new tomb, in which no one had yet been buried. So they laid Jesus there because of the Jewish preparation day; for the tomb was close by.

MATTHEW 27:57-60 — When it was evening, there came a rich man from Arimathea named Joseph, who was himself a disciple of Jesus. He went to Pilate and asked for the body of Jesus; then Pilate ordered it to be handed over. Taking the body, Joseph wrapped it [in] clean linen and laid it in his new tomb that he had hewn in the rock. Then he rolled a huge stone across the entrance to the tomb and departed.

Easter Mysteries

1. The Mystery of the Resurrection of the Lord

Lord Jesus, grant that we may always live and rejoice in our commitment to the Pascal Mystery.

LUKE 24:36-41 — While they were still speaking about this, he stood in their midst and said to them, "Peace be with you." But they were startled and terrified and thought that they were seeing a ghost. Then he said to them, "Why are you troubled? And why do questions arise in your hearts? Look at my hands and my feet, that it is I myself. Touch me and see, because a ghost does not have flesh and bones as you can see I have." And as he said this, he showed them his hands and his feet. While they were still incredulous for joy and were amazed, he asked them, "Have you anything here to eat?"

2. The Ascension: the Glorification of the Lord Jesus Fulfilled

Lord, in You and with You, bring us to the heavenly Father.

LUKE 24:50-52 — Then he led them [out] as far as Bethany, raised his hands, and blessed them. As he blessed them he parted from them and was taken up to heaven. They did him homage and then returned to Jerusalem with great joy,

3. **The Spirit: Gift of the Resurrected Christ to His Church**

Lord Jesus, grant that our lives may be animated by Your Holy Spirit.

JOHN 19:30 — When Jesus had taken the wine, he said, "It is finished." And bowing his head, he handed over the spirit.

JOHN 20:19-23 — On the evening of that first day of the week, when the doors were locked, where the disciples were, for fear of the Jews, Jesus came and stood in their midst and said to them, "Peace be with you." When he had said this, he showed them his hands and his side. The disciples rejoiced when they saw the Lord. [Jesus] said to them again, "Peace be with you. As the Father has sent me, so I send you." And when he had said this, he breathed on them and said to them, "Receive the holy Spirit. Whose sins you forgive are forgiven them, and whose sins you retain are retained."

4. **The Joy of the Virgin Mary in the Resurrection of Her Son**

Together with Mary, let us live the joy of the resurrection.

ACTS 1:14 — All these devoted themselves with one accord to prayer, together with some women, and Mary the mother of Jesus, and his brothers.

5. **The Life of the Resurrected Christ in the Church Today**

In the Word, the sacraments and the community, we meet our risen Lord.

MATTHEW 28:16-20 — The eleven disciples went to Galilee, to the mountain to which Jesus had ordered them. When they saw him, they worshiped, but they doubted. Then Jesus approached and said to them, "All power in heaven and on earth has been given to me. Go, therefore, and make disciples of all nations, baptizing them in the name of the Father, and of the Son, and of the holy Spirit, teaching them to observe all that I have commanded you. And behold, I am with you always, until the end of the age."

St. John Eudes' Unique Rosaries

The following devotions also use beads, although not the traditional Rosary beads. You might say they are more like Chaplets. However, Father Eudes presented them as Rosaries, since they focus our minds and prayers on the life of our Savior, and help us to develop healthy and beautiful dispositions and attitudes toward Jesus and Mary.

Rosary of the Eternal Father

In addition to your annual retreat, it is beneficial to set aside one day in each month — for example, the first Thursday or any other special day — to renew and stimulate the good desires and resolutions adopted in the yearly retreat. This time is also useful to make reparation for your failures in God's service and love during the month. You should apply yourself particularly to God on that day, performing all your ordinary actions with more than ordinary attention and perfection, giving yourself with special care and fervor to exercises of praise and love of Jesus. That is why I insert here various exercises and rosaries of praise, glory, and love for Jesus, which you may use on this day of retreat, selecting now one, now another, according to the graces God may give you.

On this monthly day of recollection devoted to a more particular love and praise of Jesus, you may say a rosary which I call *the Rosary of the Father of Jesus*, because it is addressed to the Eternal Father, and beg Him to praise and glorify His Son Jesus in you and for you.

This rosary is made up of thirty-four small beads, in honor of the thirty-four years of Our Lord's life on earth.

First, while holding the cross, say three times

Veni Pater Jesu,
Or "Come, Father of Jesus,"

to invoke and draw down to you the Father of Jesus, and to give yourself to Him that He may destroy all in you that is contrary to the glory of His Son, and glorify Him in you according to His holy will.

Then on each small bead say:

Pater clarifica Filium Tuum, ut Filius Tuus clarificet Te:
Or "Father, glorify your Son, that your Son may glorify you"
(John 17:1)

JOHN 17:1 — When Jesus had said this, he raised his eyes to heaven and said, "Father, the hour has come. Give glory to your son, so that your son may glorify you,

This is the prayer which the Son of God addressed to His Eternal Father on the eve of His death. Therefore, no prayer can be said by you that is more pleasing to Him than this invocation, nor can you ask Him anything that would please Him more than what you request of Him in this perfect prayer. But when you recite this invocation, remember that it came forth from the heart and lips of Jesus. Unite yourself with the humility, the purity, the love, and all the holy dispositions and intentions with which Jesus Christ uttered it, begging the Eternal Father to glorify His Divine Son throughout the whole world, and to destroy in you and in all mankind everything that is contrary to His glory. Implore Him to implant in your soul all the graces and virtues required for His perfect glorification, and to exert the power of His own zeal and love for His Son to glorify Him there, according to, His holy will.

On the large beads say:

Gloria tibi, Domine Jesu, qui natus es de Virgine,
Or "Glory to, You, Lord Jesus, Who was born of the
Virgin Mary."

When you say this, offer to Jesus Christ all the glory that ever has been, is now and ever shall be rendered to Him forever in heaven and on earth.

Rosary of Jesus and Mary

You should earnestly desire that the last words you utter in life should be: *Jesus, Mary.*

In order to dispose yourself to obtain this grace from divine mercy, it would be a good thing to end each day with the recitation of this very brief rosary, which I call the *Rosary of Jesus, Maria*, because it is composed of these two words alone:

> *Jesus, Maria* (The names of Jesus and Mary in Latin)
> Or "Jesus, Mary."

These Holy Names contain all that is greatest and most admirable in heaven and on earth, together with the entire virtue and sanctity of the most excellent prayers and devotions that could possibly be practiced.

This rosary is made up of thirty-four small beads in honor of Christ's thirty-four years on earth, and in honor of Mary's participation in them and the honor she gave Him always.

To begin, while holding the cross you may say three times

> *Veni Domine Iesu:*
> Or "Come Lord Jesus,"

with the intentions suggested for the Rosary of the Glory of Jesus, which may be found earlier in this book.

On each small bead you may pronounce the words

> *Jesus, Maria,*
> Or "Jesus, Mary,"

trying to say each with all the love and devotion you would want to have if you were at the hour of death, and as if it were the last word you should ever utter. Your intention should be to pronounce each name with all the love, or in union with all the love (for these two terms mean but one thing), which ever was offered or shall be offered forever in heaven and on earth to Jesus and Mary. You should give them this totality of love as something of your own, since, as has been said, everything belongs to you, making the offering in satisfaction for all your failures to love and serve them during your life.

On the large beads you may say the words:

Benedicta tu in Mulieribus et benedictus fructus ventris tui, Jesus:

> Or "Blessed are you among women and
> blessed is fruit of your womb, Jesus."

As you say them, offer to Jesus and Mary all the praises and blessings that ever were, are, or shall be given to Him forever on earth and in heaven, in reparation for your failures to bless and glorify them.

Rosary of the Glory of Jesus

This rosary is made up of three decades and four beads, a total of thirty-four small beads, in honor of the thirty-four years of Christ's life on earth.

First, while holding the cross, you may repeat three times

Veni Domine Jesu,

Or "Come Lord Jesus" (Revelation 22:20)

REVELATION 22:20 — The one who gives this testimony says, "Yes, I am coming soon." Amen! Come, Lord Jesus!

These are the inviting words with which St. John ends the book of Revelation, and you say them to invoke Jesus and draw Him into your soul, your mind and your heart, imploring Him to enter into you and annihilate everything in you that displeases Him, and to fill you with His grace, His spirit and His pure love. It is also a good thing to recite these same words with the same intention at the beginning of your other prayers and acts.

On each small bead say:

Gloria tibi, Domine Jesu, qui natus es de Virgine, cum Patre et Sancto Spiritu in sempiterna saecula:

Or "Glory to you, Lord Jesus, Who was born of the Virgin. Glory with the Father and the Holy Spirit forever and ever."

As you repeat this invocation you should offer to Jesus all the glory given to Him in each year of His life by His Father, His Holy Spirit and His Blessed Mother, and all His angels and saints, by way of satisfaction for your faults against Him in each year of your life, imploring Him to consecrate all that ever occurred in your life to the honor of all that took place in each year of His own.

For example, at the first bead, as you say *Gloria tibi Domine Jesu,* etc...., you should offer to Jesus all the glory of the first year of His life in satisfaction for your deficiencies in honoring Him during the first year of your life. So too you should offer Him your first year, imploring Him to cause all that occurred in it to be consecrated to the honor of all that occurred in the first year of His life.

At the second bead, you should offer Him all the glory given Him in the second year of His life by His Father, etc., while also offering Him the second year of your own life, imploring Him, to cause all that occurred in it to be consecrated to the honor of all that occurred in the second year of His life. And so on, with the other beads.

On the large beads, you say the *Gloria Patri* (Glory Be...), and as you do so, offer to the Holy Trinity all the glory that Jesus ever gave or ever shall give to the Three Divine Persons, by way of satisfaction for your faults against the Blessed Trinity.

Rosary of the Holy Love of Jesus

This rosary consists of three decades and four beads, a total of thirty four small beads, in honor of the thirty-four years of the life of Our Lord on earth, a life all of love.

To start with, while holding the cross you say

> *Veni sancte Spiritus, reple tuorum corda fidelium, et tui amoris in eis ignem accende*: "
> Or "Come, Holy Spirit, fill the hearts of Your faithful and enkindle in them the fire of Your Love."

This invocation draws down upon you the holy love of Jesus, which is His Holy Spirit, and gives you to Him that He may destroy everything in you that opposes Him, and may perfect the love of the Holy Spirit for the Son of God.

On each small bead, you say the following words, taken partly from the Gospel and partly from St. Augustine, who repeats St. Peter's triple repetition of *Amo te* to Our Lord after His resurrection, when asked whether he loved Him.

> *Amo te, amantissime Jesu; amo te bonitas infinita, amo te ex toto corde meo, ex tota anima mea, et ex totis viribus meis, et magis atque magis amare volt*:
> Or "I love You, Most Lovable Jesus,
> I love You, O Infinite Goodness,
> I love You with my whole heart and with all
> my might. I desire ever to love You more and more!"

The first

> *Amo te,*
> Or "I love you,"

should be said in union with all the love of the Eternal Father for His Son.

The second should be said with the intention of sharing all the love of the Son of God for Himself.

The third should be recited with all the love of the Holy Spirit for Jesus, bearing in mind that, in giving you His Son, the Eternal Father gave you everything with Him, as St. Paul says (Rom. 8:32), and it follows that the love of the Father, the Son, and the Holy Spirit belongs to you, and that you are entitled to employ it in order to love Jesus.

40

As you say

> *ex toto corde meo,*
> Or "with all my heart,"

you must understand by this the Heart of Jesus, the Heart of Mary, the heart of each of the angels and saints in heaven, all comprising a tremendous Heart one with the most Sacred Heart of Jesus and of Mary, by virtue of the union existing between all hearts. And this is likewise your heart, for St. Paul assures you that all things, without exception, belong to you: *omnia vestra sunt* (I Corinthians 3:22).

Consequently in loving Jesus you can and must use this universal Heart as if it were your own.

The words

> *ex tota anima mea,*
> Or "with my whole soul,"

denote the holy soul of Jesus, that of the Blessed Virgin, and all the holy souls in heaven which together form one single soul by virtue of the union wrought by charity. This soul is yours, and you must make use of it to love Him who gave it to you.

When you say:

> *ex totis viribus meis:*
> Or "with all my might,"

you ought to have the intention of employing all the powers of the divinity and humanity of Jesus and all the strength of all the creatures in heaven, on earth and even in hell, as your own power to love Jesus.

When you say the last words:

> *Et magis atque magis amare volo:*
> Or "and I desire to love You ever more and more,"

you should have the intention of employing all your will in desiring to love Jesus, and also of exerting the full extent and infinite capacity of the divine will in order to desire to love Jesus with a will that is infinite and worthy of Him, since your own natural will is not capable of loving Him as He deserves.

On the large beads of the rosary say these words of St. Augustine:

> *O ignis, qui semper ardes et numquam extinguerit, O amor! qui semper ferves et numquam tepescis, accende me, accende me totus, ut totus diligam te:*

Or "O fire, who is ever burning and never extinguished, O love, who is ever fervent and never grows cold, enkindle me, set me on fire, that I may be all aflame with love for You."

Or else, instead of this, you may say:

Veni sancte Spiritus, reple tuorum corda fidelium, et tui amoris in eis ignem accende:
Or "Come, Holy Spirit, fill the hearts of Your faithful and enkindle in them the fire of Your Love."

I might also add at this point that it is sometimes very beneficial to recite the above words after Holy Communion:

Amo te, amantissime Jesu; amo te bonitas infinita, amo te ex toto corde meo, ex tota anima mea, et ex totis viribus meis, et magis atque magis amare volt:
Or "I love You, Most Amiable Jesus, I love You, O Infinite Goodness, I love You with my whole heart, and with all my might, and I desire ever to love You more and more!"

At the moment just after Holy Communion you possess within yourself most intimately the love of the Father and of the Son and of the Holy Spirit, with the divine Heart and holy soul of Jesus, and all the powers of His divinity and humanity. You are then more than ever entitled to direct all these infinite powers as your own in loving Jesus. Then you can indeed say to Him truly

Amo te, amantissime Jesu; amo te bonitas infinita, amo te ex toto corde meo, ex tota anima mea, et ex totis viribus meis, et magis atque magis amare volt:
Or "I love You, Most Amiable Jesus, I love You, O Infinite Goodness, I love You with my whole heart, and with all my might, and I desire ever to love You more and more!"

with the intentions you have given above.

It is also a good thing to repeat, after Communion, this verse of the Psalmist:

Benedic anima mea Domino, et omnia quae intra me sunt, nomini sancto ejus:
Or "Bless the Lord, O my soul: and let all that is within me bless His holy name" (Psalm 103:1).

By this you refer to Jesus, Who is at that time within your heart as the soul of your soul, to the Most Holy Trinity, and all the wonders of heaven and earth. For they are within you in the Holy Eucharist, which is a compendium of God's wonders. And you should desire that everything within you may be employed in blessing, glorifying and loving Jesus and the Most Holy Trinity, and all the plenitude of the divinity that dwells in Jesus Christ.

Rosary of the Blessed Trinity

During a time devoted to the commemoration of the day of your baptism in the Name of the Most Holy Trinity, it would be a good thing to pay particular honor to that great mystery by saying the Rosary of the most Holy Trinity, which is made up of three decades and three beads in honor of the Three Divine Persons.

First, while holding the cross say three times the words:

> *Veni Sancta Trinitas*:
> Or "Come, Holy Trinity,"

to invoke in your memory, understanding, and will, the Father, Son and Holy Spirit, to give yourself to Them, that They may glorify Themselves in you as They will.

On each small bead, say the

> *Gloria Patri...*:
> (Glory be to the Father...),

offering to the Father, Son and Holy Spirit all the glory that has been rendered to Them from all eternity by Their own Divinity and all that shall be rendered to Them for all eternity in heaven and on earth, by way of satisfaction for the faults you have committed against Their honor.

On the large beads, say, with the same intention, the words:

> *Tibi laus, tibi gloria, tibi amor, O beata Trinitas*:
> "Praise be to You, glory to You, love to You, O Blessed Trinity."

ADDENDA

A Note on the Translators

In late 1941, the young **Thomas Merton** left his existence in the world to seek the freedom of cloistered life.

Thomas Merton

At the Trappist Abbey of Our Lady of Gethsemani novices were immersed in work and silence for two years before beginning serious study. Because of his mastery of language, one assignment given to the young frater (as novices were then called) was to translate certain spiritual classics from French. During Lent of 1943, he was given *The Life and Kingdom of Jesus* by St. John Eudes with an aggressive deadline for completion. His early autobiography describes the harrowing work:

> "After the Conventual Mass, I would get out book and pencil and papers and go to work at one of the long tables in the novitiate scriptorium, filling the yellow sheets as fast as I could, while another novice took them and typed them as soon as they were finished."[1]

Despite this pressure from the publisher, the project was completed on time. Merton's superior called the finished product "the best translation of any of the works of St. John Eudes that he had seen."[2] Archbishop Fulton Sheen agreed in his introduction to this edition of *The Kingdom*, exulting that the spiritual treatise was "now so ably translated into English."[3]

This took place years before Merton's "Seven Storey Mountain" was released to the public, so his name did not yet hold great value to the publishers. In the spirit of humility and silence, Merton accepted for his translation to be attributed simply to "A Trappist Father in The Abbey of Our Lady of Gethsemani."[4]

Steven S. Marshall is a specialist in the spiritual heritage of St. John Eudes. His book, *A Heart on Fire: St. John Eudes, Model of the New Evangelization,* has been translated into three languages and is sold worldwide. He blogs (doctorcordis.com) about spirituality. He is actively collaborating with the Vatican commission which is evaluating St. John Eudes as a candidate to be proclaimed a Doctor of the Church.

Steven S. Marshall

He holds a MA in Spiritual Theology from St. John's Seminary. Highest honors were awarded to his thesis: "Eudist Brothers: Living Communion Ecclesiology 'Before it was Cool.'" For a year he lived in Normandy, France as one of 15 people in a specialized program of spirituality studies. There, he walked in the footsteps of St. John Eudes and sat at the feet of spiritual masters from around the world. He now serves as translator and theologian for the US Region of the Eudists and lives with his wife in Southern California.

---

1   Thomas Merton, *The Seven Storey Mountain* (New York: Harcourt, Brace & Company, 1948), 401.

2   Benjamin Clark, OCSO, "Thomas Merton's Gethsemani: Part 1, the Novitiate Years," *The Merton Annual, vol. 4* (1991): 250.

3   Fulton J Sheen, Introduction to *The Life and Kingdom of Jesus in Christian Souls,* by St. John Eudes (New York: PJ Kennedy & Sons, 1946), xix.

4   The attribution to a "Trappist *father*" is curious given that Merton would not be ordained until 1949. However, there is no doubt that the work is his. Fr. Benjamin Clark OCSO was the "other novice" referred to in the Seven Storey Mountain. Fr. Clark recalls:
> "I remember one such assignment which Merton records (SSM, p. 401). Gethsemani had entered a contract to translate the work of St. John Eudes for the publication of a new edition. Several of the monks had been assigned volumes to translate, and Merton was given The Kingdom of Jesus in Christian Souls. The publishers had allowed only a short time for the work to be completed and so I was assigned to help Merton meet the deadline. I typed the finished copy in triplicate as Merton dashed off the original on sheets of yellow paper." "Thomas Merton's Gethsemani," p. 249.

About St. John Eudes

Born in France on November 14, 1601, St. John Eudes' life spanned the "Great Century." The Age of Discovery had revolutionized technology and exploration; the Council of Trent initiated a much-needed reform in the Church; among the common people, it was the dawn of a golden age of sanctity and mystic fervor.

His Spiritual Heritage

No fewer than seven Doctors of the Church had lived in the previous century. Great reformers like St. Francis de Sales, St. Teresa of Avila, and St. John of the Cross had left an indelible mark on the Catholic faith. Their influence was still fresh as St. John Eudes came onto the scene.

He was educated by the Jesuits in rural Normandy. He was ordained into the Oratory of Jesus and Mary, a society of priests which had just been founded on the model of St. Philip Neri's Oratory in Rome. The founder was Cardinal Pierre de Bérulle, a man renowned for his holiness and named "the apostle of the Incarnate Word" by Pope Urban VII. Rounding out St. John Eudes' heritage is the influence of the Discalced Carmelites. His spiritual director, Cardinal Bérulle himself, had brought sisters from St. Teresa of Avila's convent to help found the Carmel in France. John Eudes would later become spiritual director to a Carmelite convent himself. Their cloister prayed constantly for his missionary activity.

His Life of Ministry

As an avid participant in a wave of re-evangelization in France, St. John Eudes' principal apostolate was preaching parish missions. Spending anywhere from 4 to 20 weeks in each parish, he preached over 120 missions across his lifetime, always with a team of confessors providing the sacrament around the clock, and catechists meeting daily with small groups of parishioners.

Early in his priesthood, an outbreak of plague hit St. John Eudes' native region and he rushed to provide sacraments to the dying. The risk of contagion was so great no one else dared to approach the victims. In order to protect his Oratorian brothers from contagion, St. John Eudes took up residence in a large empty cider barrel outside of the city walls until the plague had ended.

His Foundations

During his missions he heard countless confessions himself, including those from women forced into prostitution. Realizing that they needed intense healing and support, he began to found "Houses of Refuge" to help them get off the street and begin a new life. In 1641 he founded the Sisters of Our Lady of Charity of the Refuge to continue this work. They would live with the penitent women and provide them with constant support. Today, these sisters are known as the Good Shepherd Sisters, inspired by their fourth vow of zeal to go out seeking the "lost sheep."

Occasionally, St. John Eudes would return to the site of a previous mission. To his dismay, he found that the fruits of the mission were consistently fading for lack of support. The crucial piece in need of change was the priesthood. At that time, the only way to be trained as a priest was through apprenticeship. The result of this training was so horribly inconsistent that the term "hocus pocus" was invented during this time to describe the corrupted Latin used by poorly trained priests during the consecration at mass. In 1643 he left the Oratory and founded the Congregation of Jesus and Mary to found a seminary. Seminary training was a radical brand-new concept which had just been proposed by the Council of Trent.

His Mark on the Church

At a mission in 1648 St. John Eudes authored the first mass in history in honor of the Heart of Mary. In 1652 he built the first church under the Immaculate Heart's patronage: the chapel of his seminary in Coutances, France. During the process of his canonization, Pope St. Pius X named St. John Eudes "the father, doctor, and apostle of liturgical devotion to the hearts of Jesus and Mary." The Heart of Jesus because he created the first Feast of the Sacred Heart in 1672, just one year before St. Margaret Mary Alacoque had her first apparition of the Sacred Heart.

Although his Marian devotion was intense from a tender age, the primary inspiration for this feast came from St. John Eudes' theology of baptism. From the beginning of his missionary career he taught that Jesus continues His Incarnation in the life of each baptized Christian. As we give ourselves to Christ, our hands become His hands, our heart is transformed into His heart. Mary is the ultimate exemplar of this. She gave her heart to God so completely that she and Jesus have just one heart between them. Thus, whoever sees Mary, sees Jesus, and honoring the heart of Mary is never separate from honoring the heart of Jesus.

Doctor of the Church?

At the time of this writing, Bishops the world over have requested that the Vatican proclaim St. John Eudes as a Doctor of the Church. This would recognize his unique contribution to our understanding of the Gospel, and his exemplary holiness of life which stands out even among saints. For more information on the progress of this cause, on his writings or spirituality, or to sign up for our e-newsletter updates, contact spirituality@eudistsusa.org.

About the Eudist Family

During his lifetime, St. John Eudes' missionary activity had three major areas of focus.

- For priests, he provided formation, education, and the spiritual support which is crucial for their role in God's plan of salvation.
- For prostitutes and others on the margins of society, he gave them a home and bound their wounds, like the Good Shepherd with his lost sheep.
- For the laity, he preached the dignity of their baptism and their responsibility to be the hands and feet of God, to continue the Incarnation.

In everything he did, he burned with the desire to be a living example of the love and mercy of God.

These are the "family values" which continue to inspire those who continue his work. To paraphrase St. Paul, John Eudes planted seeds, which others watered through the institutions he founded, and God gave the growth. Today, the family tree continues to bear fruit:

The *Congregation of Jesus and Mary* (CJM), also known as The Eudists, continues the effort to form and care for priests and other leaders within the Church. St. John Eudes called this the mission of "teaching the teachers, shepherding the shepherds, and enlightening those who are the light of the world." Continuing his efforts as a missionary preacher, Eudist priests and brothers "audaciously seek to open up new avenues for evangelization," through television, radio, and new media.

The *Religious of the Good Shepherd* (RGS) continue outreach to women in difficult situations, providing them with a deeply needed place of refuge and healing while they seek a new life. St. Mary Euphrasia drastically expanded the reach of this mission which now operates in over 70 countries worldwide. A true heiress of St. John Eudes, St. Mary Euphrasia exhorted her sisters: "We must go after the lost sheep with no other rest than the cross, no other consolation than work, and no other thirst than for justice."

In every seminary and House of Refuge founded by St. John Eudes, he also established a *Confraternity of the Holy Heart of Jesus and Mary* for the laity, now known as the Eudist Associates. The mission he gave them was twofold: First, "To glorify the divine Hearts of Jesus and Mary... working to make them live and reign in their own heart through diligent imitation of their virtues." Second, "To work for the salvation of souls... by practicing, according to their abilities, works of charity and mercy and by attaining numerous graces through prayer for the clergy and other apostolic laborers."

The *Little Sisters of the Poor* were an outgrowth of this confraternity. St. Jeanne Jugan was formed as a consecrated woman within the Eudist Family. She discovered the great need for love and mercy among the poor and elderly and the mission took on a life of its own. She passed on to them the Eudist intuition that the poor are not simply recipients of charity, they provide an encounter with Charity Himself: "My little ones, never forget that the poor are Our Lord... In serving the aged, it is He Himself whom you are serving."

A more recent "sprout" on the tree was founded by Mother Antonia Brenner in Tijuana, Mexico. After raising her children in Beverly Hills and suffering through divorce, she followed God's call to become a live-in prison minister at the *La Mesa* penitentiary. The *Eudist Servants of the 11th Hour* was founded so that other women in the latter part of their lives could imitate her in "being love" to those most in need.

The example St. John Eudes set for living out the Gospel has inspired many more individuals and organizations throughout the world. For more information about the Eudist family, news on upcoming publications, or for ways to share in our mission, contact us at spirituality@eudistsusa.org.

More than Just 50 Beads: Rosary Meditations for the Liturgical Year

These are excerpts from *The Life and the Kingdom of Jesus: A Treatise on Christian Perfection for Use by Clergy or Laity,* translated from French by Thomas Merton in The Abbey of Our Lady of Gethsémani and published by Kennedy & Sons in New York, 1946.

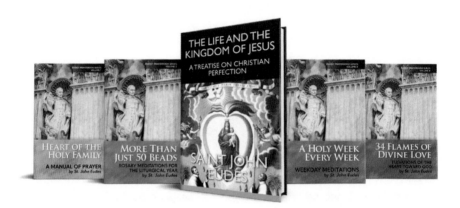

The Life and the Kingdom of Jesus as well as other titles in this series, *Heart of the Holy Family, A Holy Week Every Week* and *34 Flames of Divine Love* by St. John Eudes can be found in the Eudist bookstore on amazon.com.

More by Eudist Press

- *A Heart on Fire: St. John Eudes, a Model for the New Evangelization*
- *Spiritual Itinerary for Today with St. John Eudes*
- *Eudist Lectionary: A St. John Eudes Reader*

Eudist Prayerbook Series
- Volume 1: *Heart of the Holy Family:*
  A Manual of Prayer
- Volume 2: *More than Just 50 Beads:*
  Rosary Meditations for the Liturgical Year
- Volume 3: *A Holy Week Every Week:*
  Weekday Meditations
- Volume 4: *34 Flames of Divine Love:*
  Elevations of the Heart Towards God

Biography
- *St. John Eudes: Worker for the New Evangelization in the 17th Century*
- *In All Things, the Will of God: St. John Eudes Through His Letters*

More by St. John Eudes
St. John Eudes' Selected Works
- *The Life and Kingdom of Jesus in Christian Souls*
- *The Sacred Heart of Jesus*
- *The Admirable Heart of Mary*
- *The Priest: His Dignity and Obligations*
- *Meditations*
- *Letters and Shorter Works*

Other Works
- *Man's Contract with God in Holy Baptism*
- *The Wondrous Childhood of the Mother of God*

Made in the USA
Columbia, SC
08 July 2018